Hydroplane Boats

By Jeff Savage

Consultant:
Mark Wheeler
Member, Board of Directors
American Power Boat Association

Capstone *press*

Mankato, Minnesota

Capstone High-Interest Books are published by Capstone Press
151 Good Counsel Drive, P.O. Box 669, Mankato, Minnesota 56002
www.capstonepress.com

Library of Congress Cataloging-in-Publication Data
Savage, Jeff, 1961–
Hydroplane boats/by Jeff Savage.
    p. cm.—(Wild rides!)
    ISBN 0-7368-2430-8
    Includes bibliographical references and index.
    Contents: Hydroplane boats—Early hydroplane boats—Designing a hydroplane boat—Hydroplane boats in competition.
    1. Hydroplanes—Juvenile literature. 2. Motorboat racing—Juvenile literature. [1. Hydroplanes. 2. Motorboat racing.]
I. Title. II. Series.
VM341.S2823 2004
623.8'2314—dc22
                                                        2003014553

Editorial Credits

James Anderson, editor; Kia Adams, series designer; Patrick D. Dentinger, book
    designer; Jo Miller, photo researcher

Photo Credits

AP/Wide World Photos/Jackie Johnston, 17; Jim Bryant, 8; Seth Rossman, cover
Hydroplane and Raceboat Museum, 10, 12, 16; Bill Taylor, 20, 28; John Blair,
    25; Julie Hooton, 6–7, 18; Owen Blavman, 14; Piston Pics
    Unlimited/Carl Holmquist, 4; Robert F. Peters, 22; Speedo, 26

1 2 3 4 5 6 09 08 07 06 05 04

Table of Contents

Learn about:

- **Hydroplane speeds**
- **Types of hydroplanes**
- **Cost of hydroplanes**

CHAPTER 1

Hydroplane Boats

Six hydroplane boats cruise side by side toward the starting line. The drivers watch the starting clocks closely. The clocks count down from 60 seconds to zero. Each driver presses hard on the foot throttle. The engines are so loud that nearby fans cover their ears. The sleek boats cross the starting line just as the zero appears on the clock. The race has begun.

The hydroplanes speed left around the first turn at 140 miles (225 kilometers) an hour. A yellow hydroplane sprays water as it moves into the lead. The spray makes it difficult for the drivers in the other boats to see. The boats shake as they speed up to 200 miles (320 kilometers) an hour.

Two boats bump together. The drivers grip the steering wheels tightly. One boat spins and flips. The boat is off the course and out of the race. The rest of the drivers go around a turn and down the straightaway.

They cross the starting line. A referee waves a flag to signal that they have completed one 2-mile (3.2-kilometer) lap of the race. But the hydroplanes do not stop. They have four more laps to go.

About Hydroplane Boats

Hydroplanes are designed to cruise above the water at high speeds. The boats have a flat bottom. A thin cushion of air forms between the bottom of the boats and the water. The boats ride above the water.

Hydroplanes are among the world's fastest boats. They can go 200 miles (320 kilometers) an hour. Jet-powered hydroplanes have sped faster than 300 miles (480 kilometers) an hour.

Hydroplane boats rise above the water when traveling at high speeds.

Miss Budweiser is a popular Unlimited Light hydroplane that has won many championships.

Types of Hydroplanes

People race two main types of hydroplane boats. These classes are called Unlimited and Unlimited Light. The two classes of boats are very similar. The main differences are the size and price of the boats.

Racing teams may spend more than $700,000 to build an Unlimited boat. Because of the cost, only about 20 Unlimited hydroplanes exist in the world.

Unlimiteds are the largest hydroplane boats. They are between 28 and 32 feet (8.5 and 9.8 meters) long.

Unlimited Lights are midsized hydroplanes. They are about 20 feet (6.1 meters) long. Unlimited Lights cost as much as $200,000 to build.

Many people come to watch races between hydroplane boats. People come to these races to cheer for their favorite racing team. *Miss Budweiser* is a popular boat. The *Miss Budweiser* team is the only Unlimited Light team to have won 13 championships.

CHAPTER 2

Early Hydroplane Boats

People first built boats about 10,000 years ago. The boats were tree trunks with seats carved into them. People have been building faster boats ever since. The first motorboats were made soon after the invention of the gasoline engine in the 1880s. Faster boats came with the invention of the jet engine in 1930.

The First Hydroplanes

Emmanuel Swedenborg built the first hydroplane boat in 1716. His boat could be raised slightly above the water with scoop-shaped oars. One person paddling with two oars powered this boat.

In 1912, Gar Wood invented the hydraulic-lift dump truck. This truck raised a bucket in the back by using fluid pressure. Wood designed and built boats that worked in a similar way. Wood learned that if a boat moved fast enough, the front of the boat could be lifted with air. The boat then created less friction against the water. With less friction, the boat moved faster.

Ted Jones was the first boat designer to use a motor with a semi-submerged propeller. The top of this propeller is partly above the water. In 1948, Jones built a boat named *Slo Mo Shun IV*. In 1950, Jones set a world speed record. The boat traveled 160 miles (257 kilometers) an hour.

Learn about:

- **Body designs**

- **Propellers**

- **Blowovers**

CHAPTER 3

Designing a Hydroplane Boat

Engine size and body shape affect the speed of a hydroplane. Designers think of ways to change these features to make boats go faster.

The Hull

The main body of a hydroplane is called the hull. The hull is hollow with a flat, wide bottom. It curves upward at the front, or the bow, of the boat.

The hull can be made of wood, fiberglass, carbon fiber, or aluminum. These materials are strong and lightweight. Hydroplanes rise into the air because of their light hulls.

Engines and Speed

Propellers force hydroplane boats through the water. Hydroplane propellers usually have three blades.

Different types of engines power the propellers. Unlimited Lights use eight-cylinder engines. Unlimited Light boats travel at speeds up to 200 miles (320 kilometers) an hour.

Most hydroplane propellers have three large blades.

Unlimited hydroplanes use the same engines that many stunt planes and helicopters use. Unlimited hydroplanes travel at speeds more than 200 miles (320 kilometers) an hour.

Accidents

Serious accidents can occur when the nose of a boat rises and the boat flips over. This dangerous flip is called a blowover. Other accidents can occur when boats bump into each other during a race.

A hydroplane driver sits inside a cockpit made from parts of a fighter jet.

Cockpit

Hydroplane boats are equipped with safety features to protect drivers during an accident. The driver's seat is enclosed in a cockpit. Most hydroplane cockpits are made with F-16 fighter jet canopies. The canopies protect drivers during crashes.

Inside the cockpit, a driver sits in a roll cage. These steel bars help protect a driver if the boat flips over. The seat is shaped to hold the driver's body. The driver is strapped down to the seat with a safety harness.

Safety Gear

Hydroplane drivers wear protective clothing. Inside of cockpits, the temperature can reach 130 degrees Fahrenheit (54 degrees Celsius). Drivers wear suits that contain water. The water keeps the drivers cool. Over the suits, drivers wear fireproof jumpsuits and flotation vests.

Drivers also wear other safety gear. Gloves, a helmet, and fireproof boots are required for any driver to participate in a hydroplane race.

Learn about:

- Race courses

- Classes and heats

- Great racers

CHAPTER 4

Hydroplane Boats in Competition

Professional hydroplane races in the United States and Canada are held each year from May to November. Hydroplane races are held in Indiana, Washington, Michigan, and California. Hydroplane racing also is popular in Australia and other countries.

Hydroplane Courses

Unlimited and Unlimited Light racecourses are oval-shaped. Unlimited ovals are between 2 and 2.5 miles (3.2 and 4 kilometers) long. Unlimited Light ovals are about half as long.

Teams prepare boats with the same engine size to race in heats.

Race Classes

Hydroplanes are divided into classes before a race. Boats are grouped by engine size and weight. Classes keep each race fair. Racers only compete against other racers with similar boats.

Most hydroplane classes are divided into heats. A heat is a group of boats that race at the same time. The winners of each heat qualify to compete in the final races.

Racers collect points at each event based on how well they race. The racer who collects the most points at the end of the season wins the national points title. The champion and other top racers earn prize money.

Hydroplane teams work hard all year. After the racing season, crews repaint the boats. They may rebuild or replace the boats' engines. Drivers, mechanics, and designers work to prepare for each season's races.

APBA Gold Cup

In 1904, the American Power Boat Association (APBA) started a yearly championship race. The winner received a trophy called the APBA Gold Cup.

From 1917 to 1933, Gar Wood won the APBA Gold Cup four times as an owner and five times as a driver. He was Unlimited hydroplane racing's first superstar.

Racers and Records

The next great hydroplane racer was Bill Muncey. Between 1955 and 1959, Muncey won two APBA Gold Cups and finished second twice. Muncey set a record by winning nine races in a row. In 1981, Muncey was killed in a blowover accident during a race in Mexico.

Chip Hanauer was another great hydroplane racer. From 1982 to 1999, Hanauer won seven points titles and a record 11 APBA Gold Cups.

Speed Records

In 1977, Ken Warby of Australia set the hydroplane speed record. Warby's boat was called *Spirit of Australia*. Warby's jet engine boat traveled 288 miles (463 kilometers) an hour. One year later, Warby broke his own record. His boat traveled 317 miles (510 kilometers) an hour.

Spirit of Australia **traveled more than 300 miles (500 kilometers) per hour.**

Russ Wicks holds the current 1-mile speed record for a propeller-powered boat. On June 15, 2000, Wicks drove the U-25 Superior Racing Team's Unlimited hydroplane on Lake Washington, near Seattle, Washington. The boat traveled at an average speed of 205 miles (330 kilometers) an hour on the 1-mile racecourse.

Hydroplane racers are always trying to set new records. Every racing season, hydroplane racing fans watch someone come close to getting their name in the record books. Many times, records are not broken. But both racing fans and drivers continue to enjoy the fast and exciting sport.

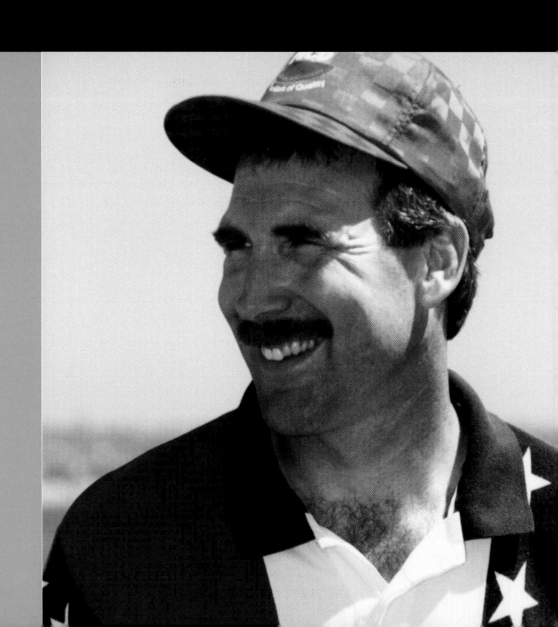

Dave Villwock

Dave Villwock is one of the most famous hydroplane racers. Villwock grew up in a racing family. His uncle Al built and raced boats. As a boy, Villwock learned about boats in his uncle's shop.

Villwock began racing at age 16. In 1989, he became a crew chief for racer Chip Hanauer's boat *Miss Circus Circus.* Three years later, Villwock raced in his first Unlimited competition in San Diego, California. Villwock won the race.

From 1998 to 2002, Villwock won 10 races in a row. His tenth win broke the record of nine wins in a row held by legendary racer Bill Muncey.

In 2003, Villwock won the General Motors Cup driving *Miss Budweiser.* It was the 41st win of his career.

Glossary

aluminum (uh-LOO-mi-nuhm)—a lightweight metal used for the frame of some boats

friction (FRIK-shuhn)—the force produced when two objects rub against each other

hull (HUL)—the frame or body of a boat

modify (MOD-uh-fye)—to change; designers modify the body or engine of a hydroplane boat to make it more powerful.

propeller (pruh-PEL-ur)—a set of rotating blades that provide the force to move a boat through the water

referee (ref-uh-REE)—someone who supervises a race

throttle (THROT-uhl)—the foot pedal in a hydroplane boat that controls the amount of fuel and air that flows into an engine; the throttle controls the boat's speed.

Read More

Bornhoft, Simon. *High Speed Boats.* The Need
For Speed. Minneapolis, Minn.: Lerner
Publications, 1999.

Cook, Nick. *The World's Fastest Boats.* Built
for Speed. Mankato, Minn.: Capstone
Press, 2001.

Useful Addresses

American Power Boat Association (APBA)
P.O. Box 377
Eastpointe, MI 48021-0377

Hydro-Prop Inc.
P.O. Box 37
4709 Crump Road, Unit #1
Lake Hamilton, FL 33851

**Unlimited Light Hydroplane Racing
Association**
12065 44th Place, South
Tukwila, WA 98178

Internet Sites

FactHound offers a safe, fun way to find Internet sites related to this book. All of the sites on FactHound have been researched by our staff.

Here's how:

1. Visit *www.facthound.com*
2. Type in this special code **0736824308** for age-appropriate sites. Or enter a search word related to this book for a more general search.
3. Click on the **Fetch It** button.

FactHound will fetch the best sites for you!

Index